Nuclear Power

by Richard Hantula

Science and Curriculum Consultant:
Debra Voege, M.A.,
Science Curriculum Resource Teacher

CHELSEA
CLUBHOUSE
An Imprint of Chelsea House Publishers

Energy Today: Nuclear Power

Chelsea Clubhouse
An imprint of Chelsea House Publishers
132 West 31st Street
New York NY 10001

Library of Congress Cataloging-in-Publication Data
Hantula, Richard.
      Nuclear power / by Richard Hantula; science and curriculum consultant, Debra Voege.
          p. cm. — (Energy today)
      Includes index.
      ISBN 978-1-60413-784-2
  1. Nuclear energy—Juvenile literature. I. Title.
TK9148.H365 2010
333.792'4—dc22 2009042794

Chelsea Clubhouse books are available at special discounts when purchased in bulk quantities for businesses, associations, institutions, or sales promotions. Please call our Special Sales Department in New York at (212) 967-8800 or (800) 322-8755.

You can find Chelsea Clubhouse on the World Wide Web at http://www.chelseahouse.com

Developed for Chelsea House by RJF Publishing LLC (www.RJFpublishing.com)
Project Editor: Jacqueline Laks Gorman
Text and cover design by Tammy West/Westgraphix LLC
Illustrations by Spectrum Creative Inc.
Photo research by Edward A. Thomas
Index by Nila Glikin
Composition by Westgraphix LLC
Cover printed by Bang Printing, Brainerd, MN
Book printed and bound by Bang Printing, Brainerd, MN
Date printed: May 2010
Printed in the United States of America

Photo Credits: 8: iStockphoto; 11: iStockphoto; 12: © Michael Ventura/Alamy; 15: © Ashley Cooper/Alamy; 17: AP Images; 18: © Tom Tracy Photography/Alamy; 21: National Archives; 25: AFP/Getty Images; 26: © kampfner photography/Alamy; 27: U.S. Navy photo by Mass Communication Specialist 2nd Class Michael D. Cole; 31: (top) iStockphoto, (bottom) © vario images GmbH & Co. KG/Alamy; 33: AFP/Getty Images; 34: © Chad Ehlers/Alamy; 36: iStockphoto; 39: Courtesy of Hyperion Power Generation; 40: Credit is given to Lawrence Livermore National Security, LLC, Lawrence Livermore National Laboratory, and the Department of Energy under whose auspices this work was performed; 41: © Steve Allen/Brand X Pictures/agefotostock; 43: Credit is given to Lawrence Livermore National Security, LLC, Lawrence Livermore National Laboratory, and the Department of Energy under whose auspices this work was performed.

10 9 8 7 6 5 4 3 2 1

This book is printed on acid-free paper.

All links and Web addresses were checked and verified to be correct at the time of publication. Because of the dynamic nature of the Web, some addresses and links may have changed since publication and may no longer be valid.

TABLE OF CONTENTS

Words that are defined in the Glossary are in **bold**
type the first time they appear in the text.

CHAPTER 1

Energy from Atoms

Energy makes things happen. It makes life possible and is involved in practically everything we do. Energy comes in different forms. Electricity is an especially important one. Electricity powers our lights, helps to heat our homes, and runs many machines. Without electricity, we would not have computers, telephones, or television.

A basic fact of nature makes it possible for us to get electricity. That fact is that energy can be changed from one form to another. Most often, we get electricity from the form of energy known as heat. Usually, the heat is used to boil water so that it turns into steam. The steam runs a machine called a **turbine**, which produces a turning movement. The turning movement causes another machine, called a **generator**, to make electricity.

Heat can be obtained in different ways. Today, the most common way to make electricity is to burn **fossil fuels** such as coal, oil, or natural gas. Another way to get heat uses a different approach. It gets heat from the energy packed inside tiny units of matter called **atoms**. This type of energy—called nuclear energy—may play an important role in providing more of the world's energy in the years to come.

Atoms and Elements

Atoms are very tiny bits of matter. They are made up of even tinier bits, or particles. These particles come in three main types.

Inside an Atom

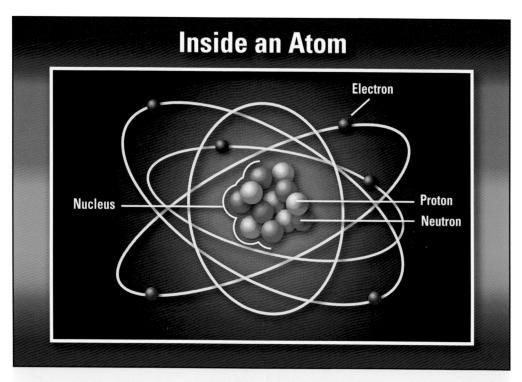

Atoms are made up of particles called protons, neutrons, and electrons. This picture shows a carbon atom.

Two—known as **protons** and **neutrons**—lie in the middle of the atom, which is called the **nucleus**. (The plural of nucleus is nuclei.) **Electrons** are the third type of particle. They fly around the nucleus. Protons tend to push each other away. This is because they all have what is called a positive electrical charge. Neutrons are neutral. This means that they do not have any charge at all. Electrons have a negative electrical charge.

What stops the nucleus from just flying apart? The answer is energy. A huge amount of energy holds the nucleus together. With certain kinds of atoms, people can make use of some of this nuclear energy. Nuclear energy, for instance, is used to make heat for producing electricity and for making powerful atomic bombs.

To produce nuclear energy, certain types of atoms are needed. Usually, they are atoms of the substances **uranium** or **plutonium**. Uranium and plutonium are both **elements**, which are basic substances that make up all matter. There are approximately 115 elements known to scientists today.

Every element has a specific number of protons in the nuclei of its atoms. The number of neutrons may vary. The nuclei of uranium and plutonium have many protons and neutrons. Uranium has 92 protons, while plutonium has 94 protons. Some elements have much smaller nuclei. Oxygen, for example, has only eight protons, carbon has six protons, and hydrogen has just one proton!

Did You Know?

Radioactivity

The nuclei of the atoms of some substances are said to be unstable. That means that every now and then, they give off **radiation**. The nature of the radiation depends on the situation and the type of substance involved. Substances that give off radiation are said to be radioactive. The radiation they give off— their radioactivity—may be harmful to living things. The elements uranium and plutonium are radioactive.

When an element gives off certain types of radiation, it changes into a different element. Scientists call this process *decay*. When a radioactive element decays, the new element may or may not also be radioactive. If it is not radioactive, the new element is said to be stable. It will not easily change into something else.

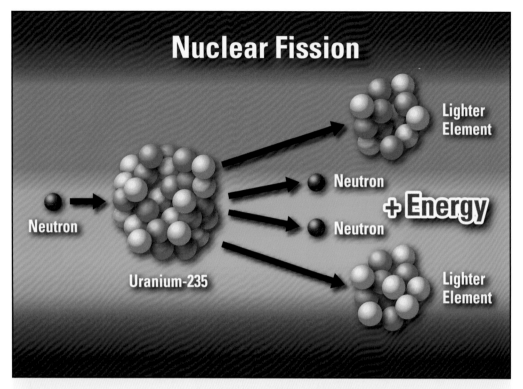

When fission of a uranium-235 atom takes place, the nucleus of the atom is split apart. This results in the release of two or three neutrons, lighter elements, and a great deal of energy.

Super Splits

Certain uranium and plutonium atoms are particularly suitable for making electricity. Their nuclei can split apart if they happen to be "hit" by a neutron. This process is called **fission**, and it results in the creation of two smaller nuclei. That is not all fission does, though. Fission also frees up one or more neutrons. In addition, it releases a huge amount of energy. In a bomb, many atoms undergo fission very quickly. The energy released shows up as heat, light, and a colossal blast. When making electricity, the fission process occurs more slowly. It takes place in what is called a nuclear reactor—a device that makes it possible to control the fission.

A nuclear power plant located in the small town of Byron, Illinois.

Enormous Energy

To really understand what happens in fission, you need to look at the mass, or amount of matter, of the particles involved. When a nucleus splits, the particles that result have less mass than the original nucleus did. In other words, some mass disappears. Actually, it gets turned into energy—a great deal of energy. The famous scientist Albert Einstein came up with a formula that described this. The formula is $e = mc^2$. Here, e is energy, m is mass, and c is the speed of light, which must be squared, or multiplied by itself. This formula can tell how much energy is produced in fission. All you have to do is multiply the amount of mass that was lost by c^2, which is a very, very big number. If you measure the speed of light in meters per second, then c is about 300 million, or 300,000,000. So c^2 is 300 million x 300 million (300,000,000 x 300,000,000), which equals 90 quadrillion (90,000,000,000,000,000)!

A reactor yields vast amounts of energy. A standard "pellet" of uranium fuel is only about as big as a fingertip, but it can produce almost as much energy as a ton of coal.

A Growth Industry

Burning fossil fuels is the most common way to produce heat to make electric **power**. It accounts for about two-thirds of the world's electricity production. In some countries, however, nuclear power is the major source of electricity. France gets about three-fourths of its electricity from nuclear power. It also provides almost as much of the electricity in Lithuania. In the United States, fossil fuels dominate, providing about 70 percent of electricity, but nuclear power is still important. The United States has more than 100 nuclear reactors. They supply about a fifth of U.S. electricity.

In 2009, there were more than 435 nuclear power reactors in approximately 30 countries around the world. They produced about 15 percent of the world's electricity. The nuclear industry

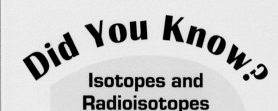

Did You Know?

Isotopes and Radioisotopes

Elements usually come in more than one version. These versions are called **isotopes**. The nuclei of their atoms differ in weight because they contain different numbers of neutrons. Take, for example, uranium. All of its isotopes have 92 protons. The common form of uranium is called uranium-238, or U-238. It has 146 neutrons. A less common, but very important, form of uranium is known as uranium-235, or U-235. It has only 143 neutrons. Isotopes that are radioactive are often referred to as radioisotopes.

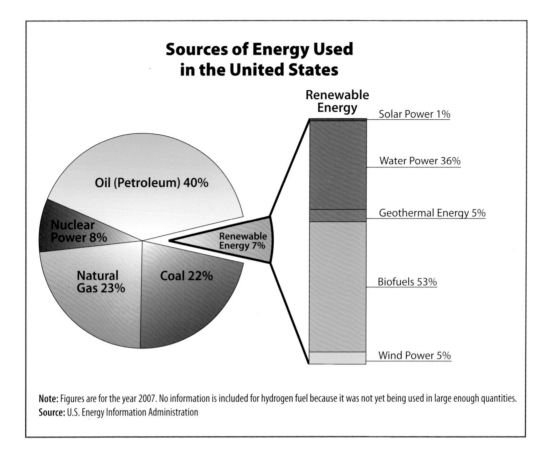

Sources of Energy Used in the United States

Oil (Petroleum) 40%

Nuclear Power 8%

Natural Gas 23%

Coal 22%

Renewable Energy 7%

Renewable Energy

Solar Power 1%

Water Power 36%

Geothermal Energy 5%

Biofuels 53%

Wind Power 5%

Note: Figures are for the year 2007. No information is included for hydrogen fuel because it was not yet being used in large enough quantities.
Source: U.S. Energy Information Administration

was growing. Nearly 50 new reactors were being built around the world in 2009, and more than 10 new reactors were planned. Also, nearly 300 additional nuclear reactors had been proposed.

This was a remarkable change from the situation in the nuclear industry several years earlier. Then, the nuclear industry seemed to be in trouble. A number of accidents associated with nuclear reactors had occurred that caused many people to be concerned about safety issues. The cost of nuclear **power plants** also caused worries. It cost a great deal of money to build new nuclear plants. It also cost a great deal to shut down, or **decommission**, old ones.

The Need for Alternative Fuels

More and more people have come to believe that the world cannot rely on fossil fuels to provide so much of our energy much longer. Coal, oil, and natural gas formed from the remains of prehistoric plants and animals that died millions of years ago. They are a relatively inexpensive and very convenient source of energy. They have many uses. They heat buildings, run cars and other kinds of vehicles, and are used to make electricity.

Fossil fuels, however, have two big drawbacks. One is that they are not **renewable**. It took millions of years for them to form, and their supply is limited. Once they are used up, they are gone. The other drawback is that burning fossil fuels emits, or releases, certain substances into the environment. Some of these **emissions** are harmful. They cause pollution that can damage the health of people or other living things. In addition, many scientists say that burning fossil fuels is causing Earth's climate to change.

There are many drawbacks associated with fossil fuels, such as the harmful emissions that enter the air when these fuels are burned.

Some of the emissions from fossil fuels, such as the gas **carbon dioxide**, help make the atmosphere (the air above Earth's surface) act somewhat like a greenhouse. It is warm inside a greenhouse because the glass roof and walls let light in and out, but tend to keep heat in. Scientists say that a similar thing happens when so-called **greenhouse gases** such as carbon dioxide collect in the atmosphere. These gases make Earth's surface get warmer. The whole planet could be affected. Ice near the North and South Poles, for example, is beginning to

Did You Know?

Nuclear Medicine

Electricity and bombs are not the only important uses of radioactive substances. Radioisotopes are valuable tools in medicine. Their radiation can be used to form a picture of the inner parts of a person's body, to help diagnose diseases or find problems. Radioisotopes also help in treating diseases. For instance, they can be used in various ways to fight cancer.

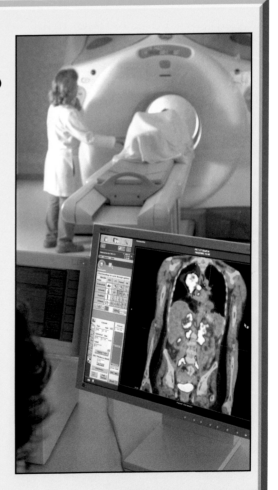

Radioisotopes help doctors get a look at internal organs so they can diagnose diseases.

melt, which would cause the oceans to rise. Islands and coastal areas may become flooded. Rainfall in other places could decrease significantly. In addition, plants and animals would have to get used to higher temperatures. Some may die.

These drawbacks have made people start to think about alternative energy sources that could replace fossil fuels. Nuclear energy is one such source. Nuclear energy is not perfect. Nuclear fuel, for example, is dangerous and has to be handled very carefully. Despite problems associated with nuclear power, though, nuclear energy has good points that make it a useful energy source. Nuclear power plants have almost no emissions. Nuclear fuel is not renewable since it is used up to produce power, but plenty of nuclear fuel is available, and more can be made in special reactors. In addition, nuclear power plants can be built almost anywhere, and they can run round-the-clock.

Other alternative energy sources have advantages of their own, but they also have drawbacks. Water power can be used only where there is the right type and amount of water. Geothermal power relies on heat deep within the ground, which means that it also can be used only in certain places. Solar power relies on the Sun's energy and does not work when the Sun does not shine. Wind power works only when the wind blows. Biofuels, such as ethanol made from plants, need to be burned, which releases emissions. In addition, a great deal of land is needed to grow the plants used to make such biofuels. In the future, it is likely that the world will continue to use a combination of different energy sources— and some people think nuclear energy may play a bigger role than it does today.

Splitting Atoms for Power

Radioactive substances found in nature give off energy in the form of radioactivity. In some cases, they may be a danger to health, but on the whole, this is not a matter of concern. Take, for instance, uranium ore. This is rock that contains uranium, so it is radioactive, but it does not release enough energy to run a generator. Also, if you pile up the ore, it will not become a bomb. Something more is needed to produce electric power or cause an explosion.

Actually, at least three things are needed for what is called "useful" fission—fission that can be used to make electricity or create an explosion. One thing is the right material. Useful fission can occur only with certain materials, one of which is uranium-235. Scientists describe such materials as fissionable. The right amount of fissionable material is also needed. There has to be enough to get the job done. These two things—the right material and right amount of it—make possible the third key requirement for useful fission. If the right amount of material is brought together under suitable conditions, a **chain reaction** can take place. The possibility of a chain reaction is what makes fissionable materials such useful sources of energy.

Chain Reaction

To see how a chain reaction works, let's look at uranium-235 (U-235). Suppose, as often happens, a free neutron—one that

Nuclear fuel is placed in fuel rods. The rods are used in the core of the reactor.

is not bound to any nucleus—is flying through the area. Suppose as well that this neutron happens to hit a U-235 nucleus. If the neutron is not moving too fast, the nucleus may capture it. This causes the nucleus to split into two smaller nuclei. In the process, some energy and two or three neutrons are released. The chain reaction can continue if one or more of these newly released neutrons happens to be captured by other U-235 nuclei. Those nuclei will then split, releasing more energy and more neutrons. As long as there are enough neutrons and enough U-235 nuclei, the process can keep going. In this way, a huge amount of energy is released.

In a bomb, the chain reaction needs to be very fast. This produces a sudden release of a great deal of energy, making the bomb explode. The situation is different in a nuclear reactor. In a reactor, the chain reaction has to occur over a long period of time. Power plants, or power stations, need a continual supply of heat to make electricity. In order to provide the right amount of heat, a reactor has ways of controlling the chain reaction. These keep the process from going too fast or too slow.

The chain reaction takes place in a part of the reactor called the core. The core is specially designed for controlling the chain

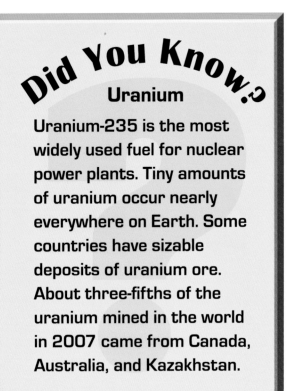

reaction. The nuclear fuel, such as U-235, is typically placed in long rods. The rods are grouped together in bundles called fuel assemblies. There are also other long rods, known as control rods, made of a material that absorbs neutrons. The control rods can be inserted into the core and removed as needed. If a chain reaction starts to go too fast, some of the control rods can be inserted. They absorb some of the neutrons flying around in the core, so that the neutrons are not available to cause atoms to undergo fission. If the reactor power needs to be increased, the control rods can be pulled out. This makes more neutrons available to cause fission.

Many reactor cores also contain a substance called a **moderator**. This slows down the flying neutrons to speeds low enough that U-235 nuclei can capture them. In some reactors, the moderator also serves as a **coolant**, keeping the core from getting too hot and melting. Many reactors use water as a moderator. Graphite is another substance that is sometimes used as a moderator.

Obtaining Nuclear Fuel

U-235 is the only fissionable form of uranium found in nature. Natural uranium, however, has very little U-235. Instead,

MARTIN HEINRICH KLAPROTH

German chemist Martin Heinrich Klaproth was born in 1743 in the town of Wernigerode. He learned chemistry while he was working for several years as an apothecary—a person who makes and sells medicines. In 1789, he discovered uranium in a mineral called pitchblende. He named the new substance for the planet Uranus, which had been discovered a few years earlier. Scientists did not yet know about radioactivity. The discovery of radioactivity came more than a century later.

In addition to uranium, Klaproth discovered the elements zirconium and cerium. When the University of Berlin was created in 1810, he became its first professor of chemistry. He died on New Year's Day 1817 in Berlin.

natural uranium is usually more than 99 percent U-238. Only about 0.7 percent is U-235. (There also may be a tiny bit of another isotope, U-234.) This level of U-235 is far too low for use in most types of reactors.

As a result, a great deal of work must be done in order to get the right type of uranium ready for use. First, uranium ore is mined. The ore contains different materials, so most of the non-uranium rock in the ore has to be removed. The result is a material often called yellowcake,

Workers at a nuclear power plant in Germany examine part of the reactor.

A technician with a barrel of yellowcake, which has been refined so that it is mostly uranium.

which is usually more than four-fifths uranium. Then, more work is needed. A process known as **enrichment** increases the amount of U-235, raising the usual 0.7 percent to whatever level is needed. For reactors, the enriched uranium material—in a form called uranium oxide—is usually shaped into little ceramic pellets. These are then put into fuel rods.

U-235 for use in nuclear reactors can be obtained in other ways as well. Some countries **reprocess** used, or spent, fuel rods. These rods no longer have enough U-235 to support a chain reaction, but they still contain some, which can be extracted and processed to make new fuel pellets.

Plutonium—more specifically, the isotope plutonium-239, or Pu-239—can also be used for nuclear fuel. (It is also used to make nuclear bombs.) Plutonium decays more rapidly than uranium. As a result, almost none can be found in nature. Instead, it is specially made from other elements. Special reactors that are used to make a great deal of nuclear fuel such as plutonium are known as **breeder reactors**.

Other types of reactor fuel also exist, and two of them will probably get more and more attention in the future. One is called MOX, which stands for Mixed OXide. MOX is a mixture of the substances uranium oxide and plutonium oxide. To make MOX, plutonium from spent (used) reactor fuel and from weapons is mixed with uranium oxide. Some countries have used MOX fuel for years. The second fuel is **thorium**-232, or Th-232. Thorium is abundant on Earth. Th-232 does not undergo fission, but it does something else that is important. When a Th-232 nucleus captures a neutron, it produces an isotope of uranium known as U-233. U-233 is fissionable, so Th-232 could be used in a breeder reactor to make U-233.

In Their Own Words

"The discovery of nuclear chain reactions need not bring about the destruction of mankind any more than did the discovery of matches. We only must do everything in our power to safeguard against its abuse."

Scientist Albert Einstein, 1953

Different Types of Reactors

There are a number of different kinds of nuclear reactors. U.S. power stations today use just two. One, called the *pressurized water reactor*, is the most common type of nuclear reactor in the world. The other type of power reactor found in the United States is the *boiling water reactor*. Both types use uranium oxide fuel. Both usually surround the core with several walls

Did You Know?

How a Generator Makes Electricity

A generator changes one type of energy—the energy of movement—into another type: electrical energy. A generator takes advantage of a few basic facts about magnets and magnetism. If you put a piece of iron (or certain other substances) near a magnet, a force will pull the iron to the magnet. The area around the magnet in which this force acts is called a magnetic field. Something interesting happens when you move a conductor (a material that can carry, or conduct, electricity) through a magnetic field. The field causes electricity—an electric current—to flow in the conductor. A current will also flow if the conductor is held steady and the magnetic field moves past it. Either of these methods may be used in a generator to produce a current.

Nuclear power plant generators usually get the movement they need from the turning movement produced by a turbine. The electric current that comes from a nuclear power plant generator switches direction many times a second. The current is known as alternating current. This is the kind of current used in the public power system, or grid.

to keep radioactive gases or liquids from getting out. The core and moderator lie inside a strong steel container called a pressure vessel. The vessel is usually located in a solid, airtight building known as a containment structure. The containment

ENRICO FERMI

Enrico Fermi was responsible for the first controlled chain reaction. Fermi was born in Rome, Italy, in 1901. He became a physics professor at the University of Rome at the age of 26. In 1938, he won the Nobel Prize—which is awarded each year for achievements in different branches of science and other areas—for his work on radioactivity and nuclear reactions involving neutrons. That same year, he moved to the United States.

During World War II, the U.S. government began a secret program called the Manhattan Project to develop the atomic bomb. Fermi played an important role in the program. As part of the project, the world's first controlled fission chain reaction took place in a reactor. Fermi headed the effort to achieve the chain reaction, which occurred on December 2, 1942. Fermi died of cancer in 1954. The element fermium was named in his honor.

A secret U.S. government program developed the atomic bomb. Two such bombs were dropped on Japan in 1945, near the end of World War II.

structure is typically made of concrete and steel. Its walls may be 3 to 6 feet (1 to 2 meters) thick. If an accident occurs in the reactor, the containment structure helps keep radioactivity from escaping into the environment.

Pressurized water reactors have two water systems. One pumps water through the reactor core under high pressure, to keep the water from boiling. The flowing water acts as a coolant. It picks up heat from the core and carries the heat to a device called a **heat exchanger**. There, the heat is transferred to the second water system. This causes the water in the second system to boil, forming steam. The steam is used to make a turbine turn, which causes a generator to produce electricity.

Boiling water reactors have just one water system. The same water that passes through the core forms the steam that drives the turbine.

Scientists in Canada invented another type of reactor known as the **CANDU reactor**. (The name comes from CANada

Did You Know?

Some Milestones in Nuclear Power

- On December 20, 1951, nuclear energy was first used to make electricity. An experimental reactor in Arco, Idaho, produced electricity to turn on four light bulbs.
- On June 26, 1954, an electricity-producing nuclear reactor was connected to a public power system for the first time. It was in Obninsk, Russia.
- On August 27, 1956, a commercial nuclear power station connected with a national grid for the first time. It was Calder Hall 1 in England.
- On December 18, 1957, the first U.S. commercial power plant began making electricity. It was the Shippingport Atomic Power Station in Pennsylvania.

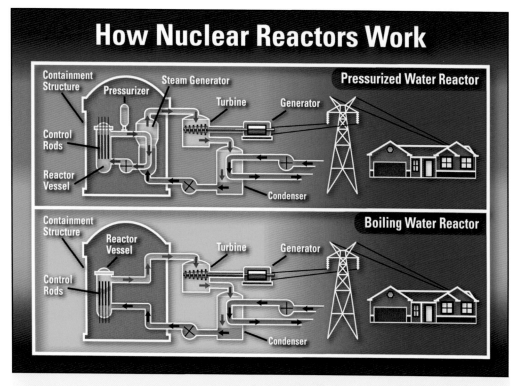

How Nuclear Reactors Work

Containment Structure
Pressurizer
Steam Generator
Turbine
Generator
Pressurized Water Reactor
Control Rods
Reactor Vessel
Condenser

Containment Structure
Reactor Vessel
Turbine
Generator
Boiling Water Reactor
Control Rods
Condenser

Fission takes place inside nuclear reactors. The heat given off turns water into steam, which turns the blades of a turbine, driving a generator that makes electricity.

Deuterium Uranium.) This type of reactor is now used in Canada as well as some other countries. It is a special kind of pressurized water reactor that uses so-called heavy water as a moderator and coolant. All water is made of hydrogen and oxygen. Ordinary water, or "light" water, uses mainly the most common hydrogen isotope. Heavy water, however, has a high percentage of a heavier hydrogen isotope called deuterium. As a result, heavy water is about 10 percent heavier than light water. Also, heavy water is a fine moderator because it is very good at slowing neutrons down for use in fission. It is so good that the CANDU reactor can use natural, unenriched uranium as fuel.

CHAPTER 3

The Case for Nuclear Power

An ideal source of energy would be low in cost and readily available. It would be safe and would not harm the environment. It would provide as much energy as people need at any time of day and on any day of the year. In addition, the energy source would continue to be reliable in the future. No current power source can satisfy all these requirements. Modern nuclear plants, however, make a reasonably good attempt.

Environment and Safety Issues

Nuclear power plants do not produce the emissions that come from burning fossil fuels. Thus, nuclear power does not contribute to the climate change or some of the other problems that have been associated with fossil fuels.

Uranium mining and related work can release polluting substances. With modern methods, however, the amount of pollutants released is small. Radioactivity is another concern about mining. Uranium ore gives off radiation, but not very much. Most of the uranium contained in the ore is U-238, which is not very radioactive.

Workers in underground mines face an extra risk. Uranium ore gives off a radioactive gas called radon. Radon is released naturally from the ground in small amounts in many parts of the world and typically disperses (scatters) in the air. In the

Open-pit uranium mines are safer for workers than underground mines.

closed-in space of an underground mine, however, radon may accumulate to a dangerous level. A good ventilation system is needed. Today, uranium mining is often done in a different way that helps avoid the danger of radon. Uranium is taken from an open pit at the surface of the ground. This allows the radon to disperse in the air.

People concerned about the safety of nuclear plants often point to the dangerous radioactivity contained in the plants. Modern plants are specially designed to prevent the radioactivity from leaking out. In addition, plant workers follow strict safety rules. Thus, while the plants do produce **radioactive waste**, much is done to keep the radioactivity away from the general environment. In addition, in many ways, the nuclear power industry has been safer and cleaner than the industries associated with other power sources, such as coal.

Power Galore

The number of people in the world keeps growing. So does the demand for electricity. The world has to find ways to supply

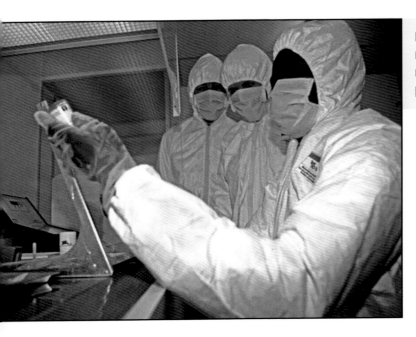

Many workers in the nuclear industry must wear special protective clothing.

more electricity. Nuclear power could be a big help since nuclear plants are capable of producing a large amount of electricity. In 2008, the world had only a few hundred nuclear plants, but they accounted for 15 percent of its electricity. There are both large and small nuclear plants. An average plant may have a capacity of 1,000 megawatts (a megawatt is a unit of measurement for the rate at which electrical energy is used). That is enough to provide electricity for hundreds of thousands of homes.

The Palo Verde nuclear power plant in Arizona has three reactors, each with a capacity about 1,200 to 1,300 megawatts. The small Fort Calhoun plant in Nebraska has a single reactor with a capacity of less than 500 megawatts. Power plants in the United States that use coal vary in capacity from a few megawatts to more than 2,000 megawatts.

People worry about running out of fossil fuels, but they do not need to worry about running out of nuclear fuels. Earth

Did You Know?

A Different Kind of Nuclear Power

Some radioisotopes are used as sources of energy for heating purposes. No chain reaction or reactor is needed. The isotopes need to be highly radioactive for this purpose, but not too radioactive. They must decay slowly enough to be useful for a long time. Plutonium-238 is often used for supplying heat in this way. Pu-238 can serve as an energy source in special places—for example, aboard spacecraft. In space, the isotopes' radiation poses no threat to living things. Each of the two U.S. "rovers" that began exploring Mars in 2004 has eight Pu-238 heater units. (For electricity, the rovers rely on solar cells and batteries.)

Radiation provides some of the power for the "rovers" exploring Mars.

does not have an endless amount of uranium, but it has a great deal. In 2007, experts believed there was enough uranium to last at least another 100 years. Building more efficient reactors will probably make the supply last much longer. Additional nuclear fuel can be gotten from the reprocessing of spent fuel and nuclear material from decommissioned weapons. Still more fuel can be obtained from breeder reactors.

Considering the Alternatives

Solar power, wind power, geothermal power, and water power are clean and renewable. Currently, the first three supply only a tiny portion of the world's electricity—approximately 2 percent in the year 2005. Water power supplies slightly more than the amount produced by nuclear power. Water power, however, is available only in certain areas.

Many people would like to see solar and wind power largely replace fossil fuels as primary sources for electricity. For that to happen, solar and wind power would have to become cheaper

Did You Know?
Floating Nuclear Plants

A floating nuclear power plant would be a handy thing. Such a plant could be assembled at a factory and then towed to wherever it was needed. Russia has plans to make several floating plants. The first, being built in St. Petersburg, may be ready for use by the year 2012. The plant will have two reactors, each with an electricity capacity of 35 megawatts. The U.S. Army did something similar years ago when it put a small reactor on an old cargo ship. From 1968 to 1975, the ship supplied power and water for a shore base in the Panama Canal Zone.

Some people worry about the safety of floating nuclear plants. They say that such plants could sink, which would pose a danger to the surrounding area, since radioactivity could be released. Critics also state that such plants would be more prone to **terrorist** attacks than land-based plants.

and more efficient. So would systems that store energy for use when there is no sunshine or wind. The International Energy Agency predicts that renewable sources such as solar, wind, and geothermal will provide only about 6 percent of the world's electricity by the year 2030. On the other hand, supporters say that nuclear power provides the best chance to meet the growing demand for electricity and cut back the use of fossil fuels.

Not Just Electric Power

Nuclear reactors do more than produce electric power and nuclear fuel. Scientists

Nuclear reactors provide the energy for huge aircraft carriers.

use them for research. They make radioisotopes for medicine and industry in reactors. Reactors also enable submarines to go at high speeds and stay underwater for weeks at a time. The heat from the reactors produces steam, which drives turbines that power the submarines. In addition, reactors make possible huge aircraft carriers, since reactors can provide a great deal of energy for long periods without refueling.

Problems with Nuclear Power

Every energy source has drawbacks. Most of the drawbacks associated with nuclear power relate to two things: safety and cost.

Protecting Against the Dangers

The fuel used in nuclear power reactors is highly radioactive. Exposure to this radiation for any length of time is dangerous. Radiation can cause burns, cancer, failure of organs in the body, and birth defects. High exposure to radiation can even kill. For this reason, nuclear fuel and things closely involved in its use must be handled with great caution. For example, fuel and other radioactive materials must always be surrounded by protective shielding, such as the pressure vessel containing the reactor core. Another important form of shielding in modern U.S. plants is the containment structure surrounding the reactor.

Most plants located in areas where earthquakes occur from time to time are designed to withstand earthquakes. If a really large quake occurs—so large that it might damage the reactor— such plants shut down automatically, to try to ensure that radioactive material is not released into the environment.

Today's power reactors have many built-in safety features. Computers and highly skilled workers keep watch over the operation of the reactor. If a chain reaction starts to go too fast, control rods can be inserted into the core to calm things down.

Radioactive material is dangerous and must be clearly labeled.

Radioactive material is dangerous and must be clearly labeled.

To protect people who work in nuclear plants, special devices monitor (keep track of) radiation levels in the plant. Workers also may wear protective clothing. In addition, to protect the public and the environment, the radiation levels of water or other substances released from the plant are monitored. Action can be taken if the levels get too high.

Plans to build a new power reactor in the United States must be approved by a U.S. government agency called the Nuclear Regulatory Commission (NRC). Before approving a new plant, the NRC takes into account comments it receives from the public. In addition, the NRC will not let a nuclear power plant start up until it is satisfied that the plant is prepared to deal with an accident.

To help protect against intruders who might want to harm reactors, plants

A workers uses special monitors to watch over the operation of a nuclear power plant.

Did You Know?

Everyday Radiation

When people worry about radiation, they are usually thinking of a certain type—ionizing radiation. We are constantly exposed to ionizing radiation, which is all around us. It comes from space in the form of the tiny particles known as cosmic rays. It is given off by radioactive elements in rocks and soil. The X-rays you get in a hospital or at the dentist's office are ionizing radiation. It only becomes a health problem when the amount a person receives gets too big.

are required to have armed guards on duty. Electronic systems also keep watch over the surrounding area, which is securely fenced in.

The transporting of radioactive materials in the United States by road, rail, air, or water is done under rules set by the NRC. Materials that are only weakly radioactive may be shipped in drums. More dangerous materials must be packed in very strong containers that are designed to not leak and not let significant amounts of radiation escape. Safeguards are also taken to protect the spent nuclear fuel while it is being transported.

All plant workers must be trained in safety procedures. They take part in regular drills intended to make sure they know what to do in the event of a disaster. The plant must also have a plan in place for handling any emergency that might affect the area outside the plant.

What to Do with Nuclear Waste

Great care must be taken with nuclear waste. Some types, however, are more dangerous than others. Most waste is only somewhat radioactive. Examples include most tools and protective clothing used by workers. These items are usually burned or buried to dispose of them. Waste that is a bit more radioactive needs to be guarded by shielding. In many cases, such waste does not stay seriously radioactive very long. Disposing of such waste often involves keeping it—enclosed in concrete—in a storage area, or repository.

Some waste is very radioactive and can stay dangerous for a long time. This high-level waste requires especially careful handling and storage. Such waste includes spent nuclear fuel and waste that is left over from the reprocessing of used nuclear materials.

This dangerous nuclear waste has to be securely stored, sealed away from any contact with people, for thousands of years or more. The most dangerous waste is currently held in

At a nuclear plant in England, barrels containing radioactive waste are stored in a pool where they are kept cool.

The containment structures around nuclear reactors provide important protection.

secure areas near reactors or at other sites. Often, it is kept at the bottom of deep ponds, below at least 10 feet (3 meters) of water. Some waste is kept, surrounded by concrete, in dry containers or rooms, with air flowing by to carry away the heat produced by the waste. Over time, the radiation and heat decrease. After about 40 to 50 years, the levels have dropped enough so that it is possible to ship the waste to a permanent, or long-term, storage facility.

Even after this time, though, high-level waste remains dangerously radioactive. So far, no country has been able to decide on a way to create a permanent storage site for the most dangerous reactor waste. Scientists have thought of many ways to handle such waste. They have considered sending it into space, placing it under the ocean floor, and even burying it in polar ice caps. Currently, many experts think high-level radioactive waste would best be stored deep underground. The place should be remote, dry, and quiet, with no known threat of earthquakes. Finding a place that meets those conditions now—and will meet them for thousands of years to come—is very hard. Plus, some communities simply oppose putting a waste-storage facility anywhere nearby. That is why no permanent storage site for high-level reactor waste has yet been set up.

Did You Know?

Chernobyl

Chernobyl in Ukraine was the site of the most serious nuclear power plant accident in history. It took place on April 26, 1986. During a test of a reactor, a power surge occurred. This led to a steam explosion that blew open the top of the reactor. Another explosion and a fire followed. The top of the reactor and the roof of the building were blown off. Workers made mistakes, and the plant was poorly designed. It did not, for example, have a U.S.-style containment structure, so there was nothing to stop radioactive material from escaping. Radioactive dust spread over areas of Ukraine, Belarus, and Russia and was carried over much of the rest of Europe.

More than 30 people at the scene died either right away or within a few months. Thousands of people living in the area were moved from their homes. According to a 2006 study, the overall death toll was more than 50. Researchers thought it was possible that thousands more people might die as a result of radiation from the accident in the future.

After the disaster, approximately 200 tons (180 metric tons) of radioactive material remained in the ruined reactor. To keep the radiation from escaping, the reactor was covered with a massive concrete "shelter." Three other power reactors at the site continued to operate. They were closed down, one by one. The last one shut down in 2000. Meanwhile, a small number of the people who had been moved from the affected area returned there to live.

Protecting Sites from Terrorists

Some of the safety measures required by the U.S. government are meant to protect against an attack by terrorists on a power plant, waste site, or shipment of radioactive material. Terrorists might try to spread radiation in order to cause deaths and create panic among the public. In an effort to protect against this, nuclear materials are well shielded, and the sites are kept under guard. Power plants are surrounded by barriers to keep a car or truck from barging in. Many nuclear experts believe that terrorists are not likely to succeed in spreading large amounts of radiation. If terrorists somehow managed to steal a container carrying radioactive waste, hoping to spread the material, they would probably die or be seriously hurt as a result of handling the waste.

The Three Mile Island power plant in Pennsylvania, the scene of the most famous nuclear accident in the United States.

Nuclear Accidents

Accidents have occurred at nuclear plants, and a small number have resulted in deaths. No matter how much care is taken, accidents do happen. One of the most famous accidents occurred in March 1979 at the Three Mile Island power plant in Pennsylvania. One of the plant's reactors had a coolant failure. Some nuclear fuel melted, and a small amount of radioactive gas was released into the air. There were no deaths or injuries. Still, the accident upset Americans, causing many to question the safety of nuclear power.

Modern reactors are designed to prevent or minimize the release of radiation. This was not always the case. In the past, some plants were built without containment structures or similar protection. A serious accident occurred in 1986 at such a plant at Chernobyl, in what is now Ukraine. Dozens of people were killed, and radioactive dust spread over a huge area of the world. More recent accidents have affected mainly workers at nuclear plants.

High Costs

Nuclear plants are very expensive to build. They often cost even more to shut down. Remote-controlled machines may be used because the radioactive materials are often too dangerous for people to handle. Authorities must seal off the plant area for years to let the radiation level die down. Then, radioactive materials need to be carefully stored away as radioactive waste when the plant is finally taken apart. All this adds up to a lot of money. People will have to weigh the costs and other problems associated with nuclear power against the need to produce clean energy for the world.

CHAPTER 5

Prospects and Plans

The nuclear power industry began with great excitement. Then, the industry stopped growing for many years because of worries about dangers and costs. Some countries cut back or shut down their nuclear industries. In the United States, planning for new nuclear plants stopped. The turning point was the March 1979 accident at the Three Mile Island power plant in Pennsylvania. More recently, the industry has started growing again.

Reactor Research

Scientists keep looking for ways to make better power reactors. Several countries have joined a program launched by the United States in 2000. The project aims to develop six types of new "fourth-generation" reactors. First-generation reactors were those used in the early days of nuclear power, in the 1950s and 1960s. Today's reactors are more modern in design and belong mostly to the second generation of reactors. If they are even more modern, they belong to the third generation.

Six types of fourth-generation reactors are being developed. These reactors will come closer to the ideal of **sustainability**. This involves making sure that people in the future will have the resources to meet their needs. As an energy source, fossil fuels are not sustainable because they are being used up. Nuclear power can be thought of as sustainable since it is possible to

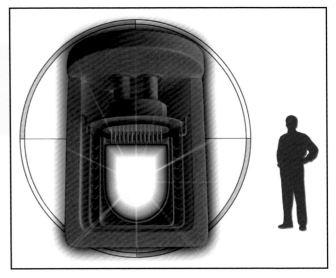

Work is going on to create compact nuclear reactors, such as this one. This type of reactor could be transported to where it was needed.

create new nuclear fuel. The people developing fourth-generation reactors have several goals. These include more efficient use of uranium, better management of nuclear waste, and increased safety and reliability. The new reactors might be ready to come into use by the year 2030 or even earlier.

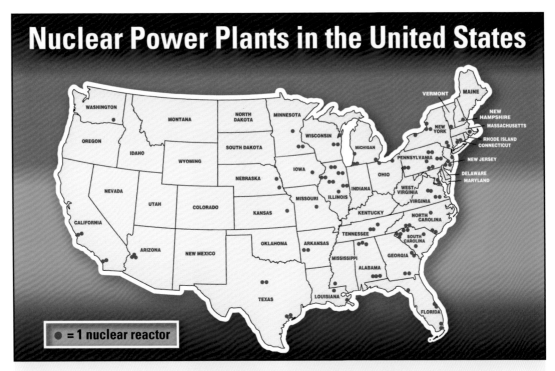

Nuclear Power Plants in the United States

● = 1 nuclear reactor

This map shows the location of nuclear reactors in the United States. These reactors supply about a fifth of the country's electricity. (There are no reactors in Alaska and Hawaii.)

All six types of fourth-generation reactors being developed today would operate at higher temperatures than current reactors. Some of the new reactors could provide heat for the production of hydrogen for **fuel cells**. Fuel cells are devices that make electricity by combining hydrogen with oxygen from the air. Many experts say that fuel cells could be a good power source for a wide range of things, from cars, boats, and spaceships to homes and larger buildings. Fuel cells are clean, their chief waste product is water, and their fuel—hydrogen—is plentiful. However, it takes a great deal of energy to obtain hydrogen from, say, water. Perhaps the new nuclear reactors will be able to supply energy cheaply enough to help make fuel cells practical.

Fusion Power

Splitting atoms—nuclear fission—is one way to get at the energy packed inside the atoms. Another way is to slam two atoms together. If their nuclei combine to form a single larger nucleus, energy is released. This process, called **fusion**, is why the

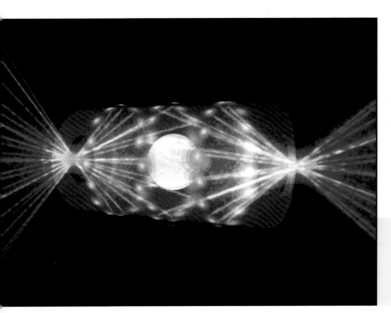

In some experiments going on with nuclear fusion, laser beams are aimed at pellets of hydrogen fuel.

Sun shines. (Nuclear fusion occurs naturally in stars, such as the Sun.) Scientists hope to make fusion into a practical source of energy on Earth. It would have a number of advantages over fission. For one thing, fusion can release much more energy than fission. For another, while it would produce some radioactive waste, it would not produce the kinds of dangerous radioactive waste that fission does. Also, the fuel it would use is hydrogen, which is quite abundant on Earth.

Fusion takes place inside the Sun because of the extremely high temperatures there. They run into millions of degrees—so hot that atoms lose their electrons. The result is something called

Did You Know?

Reprocessing

Recycling can make it easier to deal with nuclear waste. In several countries, used fuel from nuclear reactors is reprocessed. This reduces the amount of high-level waste that needs to be stored. Reprocessing methods can use almost all of the uranium and plutonium in spent fuel. The plutonium may be used in breeder reactors or mixed with uranium in MOX fuel.

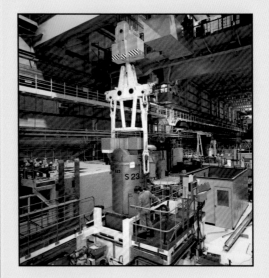

A nuclear reprocessing plant.

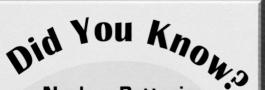

Nuclear Batteries

A miniature nuclear plant—which can be looked at as a type of nuclear battery—could come in handy in remote areas that need electricity. Several groups are exploring the idea. One is the Japanese company Toshiba. Its mini-nuclear plant would be buried deep underground. The plant would run for 30 years or so before it would need to be refueled or replaced.

plasma—a sort of gas in which electrons are separated from atoms. The nuclei in the plasma move about at terrific speeds. Normally, the nuclei—which are all positively charged—would be expected to push each other away. Inside the Sun, though, nuclei slam into each other with such speed that they fuse together.

Creating conditions like this on Earth takes enormous energy. Energy is needed not only to heat the fuel but also to keep the hot nuclei from flying away. Inside the Sun, this job of confining the nuclei is done by the Sun's gravity. On Earth, scientists have tried different methods to confine the nuclei. So far, none of the methods has fully succeeded, but scientists continue to work on fusion.

Looking Ahead

It is becoming more and more important to find alternatives to fossil fuels. Nuclear fission may be one of those alternatives. It is a practical energy source, it is available now, and people have a great deal of experience using it. Will its use increase in the future? That depends on how it will compare to other energy sources, especially regarding cost and safety.

Did You Know?

Mega Machines

Scientists studying fusion have to deal with superhot hydrogen plasma. They use huge machines for this. One method tries to contain the plasma with magnetic fields. The biggest machine for doing this is being built in Cadarache, France. It is called the International Thermonuclear Experimental Reactor, or ITER. Work on the site began in 2007. If all goes as planned, experiments will begin by 2018. ITER will use a structure called a tokamak for the magnetic field. The building containing the tokamak will be 187 feet (57 meters) high and go 56 feet (17 meters) under the ground.

The other main fusion method shoots powerful laser beams at a tiny pellet of hydrogen fuel. The world's largest and highest-energy laser system will be used for this. It can shoot 192 laser beams at a target. The system is housed in a huge building, called the National Ignition Facility. The building is located at the Lawrence Livermore National Laboratory in California.

The National Ignition Facility was dedicated in May 2009.

atom: A unit of matter that has a nucleus (middle) containing one or more positively charged particles called protons along with, in most cases, particles called neutrons that have no charge. One or more negatively charged electrons surround the nucleus.

breeder reactor: A type of reactor that can produce more fissionable material than it consumes.

CANDU reactor: A type of reactor developed in Canada that uses heavy water as a moderator and can even use natural, unenriched uranium as fuel.

carbon dioxide: A gas formed when fossil fuels are burned; also written as CO_2.

chain reaction: A reaction that, once started, continues on its own.

coolant: Something that cools and may prevent overheating in a device.

decommission: To remove a reactor or weapon from service.

electron: A small, negatively charged particle in an atom, found outside the nucleus.

element: A basic chemical substance that cannot be divided into simpler substances.

emission: A substance that is released into the air.

energy: The ability to do work.

enrichment: The process of increasing the percentage of uranium-235 in uranium and decreasing the percentage of uranium-238.

fission: Splitting an atomic nucleus into two smaller ones.

fossil fuel: A fuel, such as coal, natural gas, or oil, that was formed underground over millions of years from the remains of prehistoric plants and animals. Such fuels are not renewable.

fuel cell: A device that uses a reaction between two substances, such as hydrogen and oxygen, to make electricity.

fusion: An energy-producing process that occurs in the Sun, involving the combination, or fusion, of atomic nuclei.

generator: A machine that is used to convert energy, such as that provided by burning fuel or by wind or water, into electricity.

greenhouse gases: Gases that trap heat from the Sun within the atmosphere; carbon dioxide is one of the most common.

heat exchanger: A device that transfers heat from one substance to another.

isotope: A form of an element with a specific number of neutrons. Some isotopes, called radioisotopes, give off radiation and thereby turn, or decay, into other isotopes or other elements.

moderator: A substance used in a nuclear reactor to slow down speeding neutrons so that they will be more likely to be captured by atoms and cause fission.

neutron: A particle found in the nuclei of atoms that has no charge.

nucleus: The central part of an atom that contains one or more protons and, in most cases, neutrons.

plutonium: A radioactive element usually made in reactors by nuclear processes.

power: The rate at which energy is used to do work. People often say "electric power" or "power" to refer to electricity; for example, nuclear power commonly means electricity produced from nuclear energy.

power plant: A place for the production of electric power, also sometimes called a "power station."

proton: A positively charged particle found in the nuclei of atoms.

radiation: Various kinds of energy given off by objects; examples include light and the harmful rays and particles given off by "radioactive" materials.

radioactive waste: Materials that give off harmful radiation, or radioactivity, and are left over from the production of nuclear power.

renewable: A resource, such as a source of energy, that never gets used up. Energy sources such as sunlight and wind are renewable. Energy sources such as coal, natural gas, and oil are nonrenewable.

reprocess: To treat used, or spent, reactor fuel in order to make use of uranium and plutonium remaining in the fuel.

sustainability: The capacity to last and not be used up. The word is often used with regard to ways of living and working that leave plenty of natural resources for the future.

terrorist: A person who uses violence for political purposes.

thorium: A common radioactive element that can be used as a source of uranium to be used in fission.

turbine: A machine that produces a turning action, which can be used to make electricity. The turning action may be caused by steam, wind, or some other energy source.

uranium: A radioactive element that is a heavy silvery-white metal.

Read these books:

Kidd, J. S., and Renee A. Kidd. *Nuclear Power—The Study of Quarks & Sparks*. New York: Chelsea House, 2006.

McLeish, Ewan. *The Pros and Cons of Nuclear Power*. New York: Rosen, 2008.

Povey, Karen D. *Energy Alternatives*. San Diego: Lucent, 2007.

Townsend, John. *Using Nuclear Energy*. Chicago: Heinemann, 2009.

Look up these Web sites:

American Nuclear Society
http://www.aboutnuclear.org

How Nuclear Power Works
http://www.howstuffworks.com/nuclear-power.htm

Nuclear Energy Student Zone
http://www.ne.doe.gov/students

Nuclear Energy Kids Page
http://tonto.eia.doe.gov/kids/energy.cfm?page = nuclear_home-basics

U.S. Nuclear Regulatory Commission: Students' Corner
http://www.nrc.gov/reading-rm/basic-ref/students.html

Key Internet search terms:

atom, atomic energy, fission, fusion, nuclear energy, nuclear power, nuclear reactor

INDEX

The abbreviation *ill.* stands for illustration, and *ills.* stands for illustrations. Page references to illustrations and maps are in *italic* type.

About the Author

Richard Hantula has written, edited, and translated books and articles on science and technology for more than three decades. He was the senior U.S. editor for the *Macmillan Encyclopedia of Science*.